Contents

What is a farm?

A farm is a place where food is grown.

World of Farming

Farm Animals

Nancy Dickmann

www.raintreepublishers.co.uk
Visit our website to find out
more information about
Raintree books.

To order:
☎ Phone 0845 6044371
🖷 Fax +44 (0) 1865 312263
✉ Email myorders@raintreepublishers.co.uk

Customers from outside the UK please telephone +44 1865 312262

Raintree is an imprint of Capstone Global Library Limited, a company
incorporated in England and Wales having its registered office at 7 Pilgrim
Street, London, EC4V 6LB – Registered company number: 6695582

Edited by Siân Smith, Nancy Dickmann, and Rebecca Rissman
Designed by Joanna Hinton-Malivoire
Picture research by Mica Brancic
Production by Victoria Fitzgerald
Originated by Capstone Global Library Ltd
Colour reproduction by Dot Gradations Ltd, UK
Printed and bound in China by South China Printing Company Ltd

ISBN 978 0 431 19553 7 (hardback)
15 14 13 12 11 10
10 9 8 7 6 5 4 3 2 1

ISBN 978 0 431 19560 5 (paperback)
16 15 14 13 12 11
10 9 8 7 6 5 4 3 2 1

British Library Cataloguing in Publication Data
Dickmann, Nancy.
   Farm animals. -- (World of farming)
   1. Livestock--Pictorial works--Juvenile literature.
   I. Title II. Series
   636-dc22

Acknowledgements
We would like to thank the following for permission to reproduce
photographs: Photolibrary pp.**4** (F1 Online/Photo Thomas Gruener), **5**
(Robert Harding Travel/Robert Harding), **6** (age fotostock/Stuart Pearce),
7 (Fresh Food Images/Gerrit Buntrock), **8** (Westend61/Gerald Staufer),
9 (Flirt Collection/Julie Habel), **10** (Ableimages/julian winslow), **11**
(Juniors Bildarchiv), **12** (Oxford Scientific (OSF)/Colin Monteath), **13**
(Superstock/Superstock Inc), **14** (First Light Associated Photographers/Brian
Summers), **15** (All Canada Photos/Steve Ogle), **16** (Tips Italia/Sergio Tafner
Jorge), **17** (age fotostock/Leonardo Diaz Romero), **18** (Geoff Higgins),
19 (Juniors Bildarchiv), **20** (Moodboard RF), **21** (Index Stock Imagery/
Henry Horenstein), **22** (Fresh Food Images/Gerrit Buntrock), **23 top**, **23
middle** (age fotostock/Leonardo Diaz Romero), **23 bottom** (Superstock/
Superstock Inc).

Front cover photograph of spring lambs grazing in a field reproduced
with permission of iStockPhoto (locke_rd). Back cover photograph of a
border collie dog, working merino sheep reproduced with permission of
Photolibrary (Geoff Higgins).

The publisher would like to thank Dee Reid, Diana Bentley, and Nancy Harris
for their invaluable help with this book.

Every effort has been made to contact copyright holders of material
reproduced in this book. Any omissions will be rectified in subsequent
printings if notice is given to the publishers.

Many animals live on farms.

Animals on a farm

Cows live on a farm.

Some cows give us milk.

Chickens live on a farm.

Some chickens lay eggs.

Pigs live on a farm.

Pigs love to roll in the mud.

Sheep live on a farm.

wool

Sheep give us wool.

Some farms have ducks.

Some farms have llamas.

Working animals

Horses can help move cows.

Oxen can help pull ploughs.

Dogs can help move sheep.

Cats can help catch rats and mice.

Taking care of farm animals

Farm animals need food and water.

Farm animals need a safe place
to sleep.

Can you remember?

Which animals give us milk?

Answer on page 24

Picture glossary

oxen cows or bulls that are trained to pull ploughs or do other farm jobs

plough farm tool that breaks up the ground so that farmers can plant seeds

wool hairy body covering on sheep. Wool can be made into clothes and blankets.

Index 2/6/11

Answer to quiz on page 22: Cows give us milk.

Notes to parents and teachers

Before reading

Ask the children if they have ever visited a farm. Do they know anyone who lives on a farm? Make a list together of all the farm animals they can think of. Ask them why they think these animals live on a farm.

After reading

• Sing "Old MacDonald Had a Farm" together. Hold up pictures of each animal to prompt the children to make the correct animal noise. During PE you could put the pictures up on the walls around the hall and when you make each animal noise the children should run to the right picture.

• Talk to the children about page 17. Do they see cows pulling ploughs in their country? What is used instead? Ask them why they think cows and horses are used instead of machines in other countries.